Jake Farriss is a sixteen-year-old school student. He loves playing guitar as well as cooking and eating. He lives in Sydney with his mother, Beth, an interior designer, and his father, Tim, a musician with INXS. **The Teenager's Survival Cookbook** is his first book.

theteenager'ssurvivalcookbook

jake farriss

PAN

Pan Macmillan Australia

contents

introduction

If you're reading this, then I should firstly say, 'Thanks for buying my book!'

It's a book that began as a year-eight project. The teacher asked us to do a presentation piece on something that we were interested in. We had three months to do it and his expectations were pretty high! Some kids created poetry books and paintings, others made model rockets, dog kennels, short films – one even made a sword – you get the idea.

But none of that was for me. I've always loved food, even as a baby, or so I've been told. The older I got, the hungrier I got, and I guess my parents found it hard to keep up catering for me as often as I wanted. So I learned to cook for myself from an early age and somewhere along the line the joy for me became about making the food as well as eating it.

Apparently most teenagers eat a lot while they're growing, so by writing a cookbook for my project I intended to help others my age cook and learn a bit about book production along the way. Between homework, my passion for music and my guitar, it was hard work, but I always have time to collect and try new recipes and I haven't had a very long life yet, so stay tuned for my next cookbook!

I've had a lot of help along the way from many inspiring people and friends, who have offered advice or recipes.

Many thanks to: Mum and Dad (Beth and Tim), for always being there for me and (sometimes) for their help. Grandma Pam and Ma Jill Farriss for their cooking 'genes'. Bryan Lynch, Dad and David Hancock for showing me how well men can cook. Uncle Martin for showing my project to the 'right' people, Baz and Melski for their valuable production assistance. Mr Andrew Hill, my teacher, for obvious reasons. Anna McFarlane for believing in my book, and Brianne and all at Pan Macmillan. And to all my friends for giving me great 'teenage' suggestions.

HAPPY MUNCHING

munchies

Egg & bacon tarts

Ever want a good bacon and eggs brekkie but don't have the time or enthusiasm to get it crankin'? Well, this is the recipe for you! MAKES 12 TARTS.

12 thin slices soft white or brown bread
12 medium-sized eggs
3 rashers bacon, chopped

1 **Preheat the oven to 180°C.**
2 **Cut the crusts off the bread.**
3 **Grease a 12-cup muffin tin and put one slice of bread in each cup. Break an egg onto the bread in each cup and then add the bacon.**
4 **Place in the oven for about 20 minutes.**
5 **Take the tarts out of the muffin tin and put on a tray in the oven for a further few minutes to brown the bottoms.**
6 **Serve straightaway.**

Home-made
bruschetta

This is the sort of thing you'd get in an expensive Italian restaurant, but it's so quick and tasty to make that the next time you get a bill with '$20 – BRUSCHETTA' on it, you can tell them where to put their – Sorry, this one is just so good! SERVES 1.

2 thick slices ciabatta bread
1 level teaspoon basil pesto
3 roma tomatoes, finely chopped
1/2 onion, finely chopped
1 pinch sea salt

1 **Toast the bread in a toaster.**
2 **Spread basil pesto on the toasted bread.**
3 **Mix the tomatoes, onion and sea salt. Pile on the bread and serve.**

Roasted
peanuts

These peanuts redefine the word 'more-ish', so this recipe is definitely one you'll be making more than once!

250 g raw shelled peanuts
100 g raw mixed nuts
1/2 cup honey
1 1/2 teaspoons Chinese five-spice powder

1 Preheat the oven to 150°C.
2 Combine the ingredients in a small saucepan and warm over low heat until all the nuts are covered evenly.
3 Spread the nut mixture onto a large baking tray lined with baking paper and bake for 15–20 minutes, or until golden brown.
4 Allow to cool before serving.

Mini muffin
pizzas

This one's a hunger punch for lunch! SERVES 1.

2 English muffins, cut in half
50 g tomato paste
1 handful grated cheese
1 small handful fresh oregano, finely chopped

SWEET TOPPING
1 small banana, peeled and sliced
1 1/2 rashers bacon

SAVOURY TOPPING
barbecue sauce
strips of barbecued chicken (you can get these at the supermarket or a chicken shop)

1 Preheat the grill.
2 Spread the tomato paste over the muffins.
3 Mix the grated cheese and oregano and set aside.

4 For the sweet topping, place the banana slices and bacon rashers on the muffins, then cover with the mix of cheese and oregano.

5 For the savoury topping, place the barbecue sauce and chicken strips on the muffins and cover with the cheese and oregano mix.

6 Place the muffins under the grill and grill for a few minutes, or until the cheese is golden brown.

Milo
toast

I know that this is on the simple side, but sometimes you just gotta feed your face fast! SERVES 1.

Milo
1 banana, peeled
2 slices of bread, toasted

1 Sprinkle a thick layer of Milo over the toast.
2 Lay the banana on the toast.
3 Gently fold the toast in half and eat like a taco.

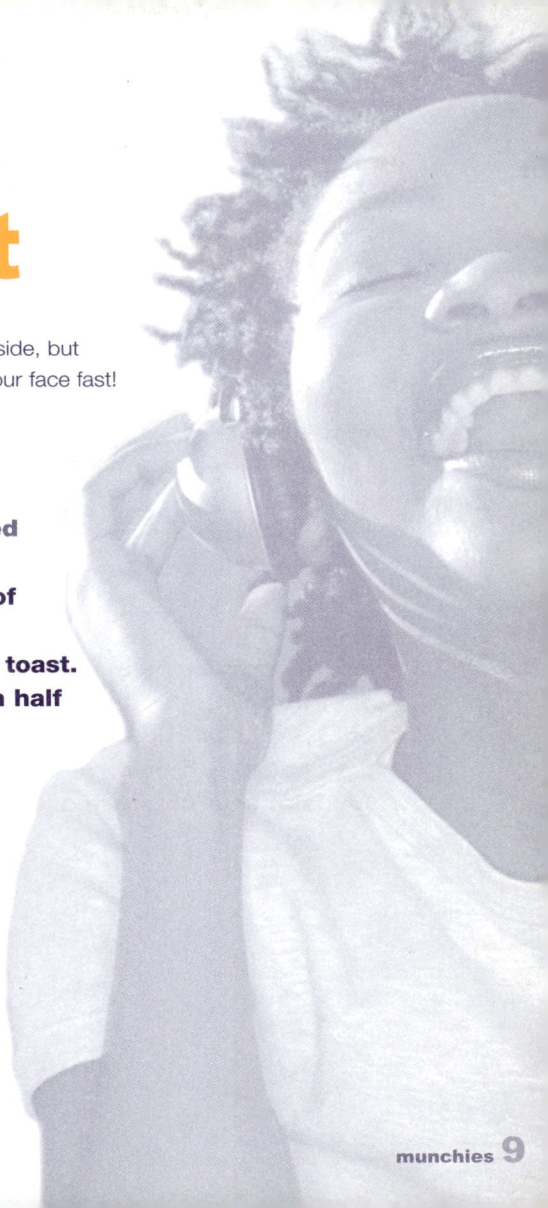

Ezy nachos

Everyone loves Mexican food and to be honest, if you find this one hard you should reconsider cooking! SERVES 1.

2 cups original corn chips
1 cup of nachos topping (you can get this at any supermarket)
grated tasty cheese
1 dollop sour cream

1 **Preheat the oven to 200°C.**
2 **Put the corn chips in a small ceramic oven-proof dish. Top with the nachos topping and cheese.**
3 **Stick the dish in the oven for 10–15 minutes, or until the cheese is brown.**
4 **Top with sour cream and serve.**

Italian-style baked beans on toast

Perfect for after school or work. It's one of those snacks that just hits the spot. SERVES 1.

1 tablespoon vegetable oil
1 onion, finely chopped
4 rashers bacon, chopped
200 g tin baked beans (or 400 g if you're really hungry!)
1 small handful whole oregano leaves
2 pieces thick toast

1 Heat a frying pan over medium heat and then add the oil.
2 Add the onion and bacon and fry for about 3 minutes, or until the onion is just beginning to brown.
3 Add the baked beans and oregano to the pan and mix. Simmer for 2 minutes, then remove from the heat.
4 Spoon the contents onto the toast, season with salt and pepper and serve.

Late-night saviour

Finally – a use for all those packets of two-minute noodles in the back of the pantry! SERVES 1.

1 packet two-minute noodles
your favourite raw vegetables, finely chopped
2 cups cous cous
2 cups boiling water
grated cheese

1 Fill the kettle and turn it on.
2 Boil a large pot of water. When boiling, add the noodles and vegetables, but not the flavour sachet from the noodles. Cook for about 2 minutes. Drain and let stand.
3 Put the cous cous in a bowl. When the kettle has boiled, add the boiling water to the cous cous and cover. Let stand for 5 minutes.
4 Drain the cous cous and add to the noodle mixture. Mix through. Then stir in the flavour sachet from the noodle packet.
5 Sprinkle cheese on top and serve.

Cajun
snack

Exotic, not toxic. What the …? You'll have to excuse me on that joke, but it's true. Trés bon! SERVES 1.

2 large crackers
1 ripe avocado
2–4 button mushrooms, chopped
Cajun spice
3–4 leaves rocket

1 Spread the avocado onto the crackers.
2 Sprinkle the Cajun spice evenly over the avocado.
3 Add the mushrooms and rocket and serve straightaway.

liquids

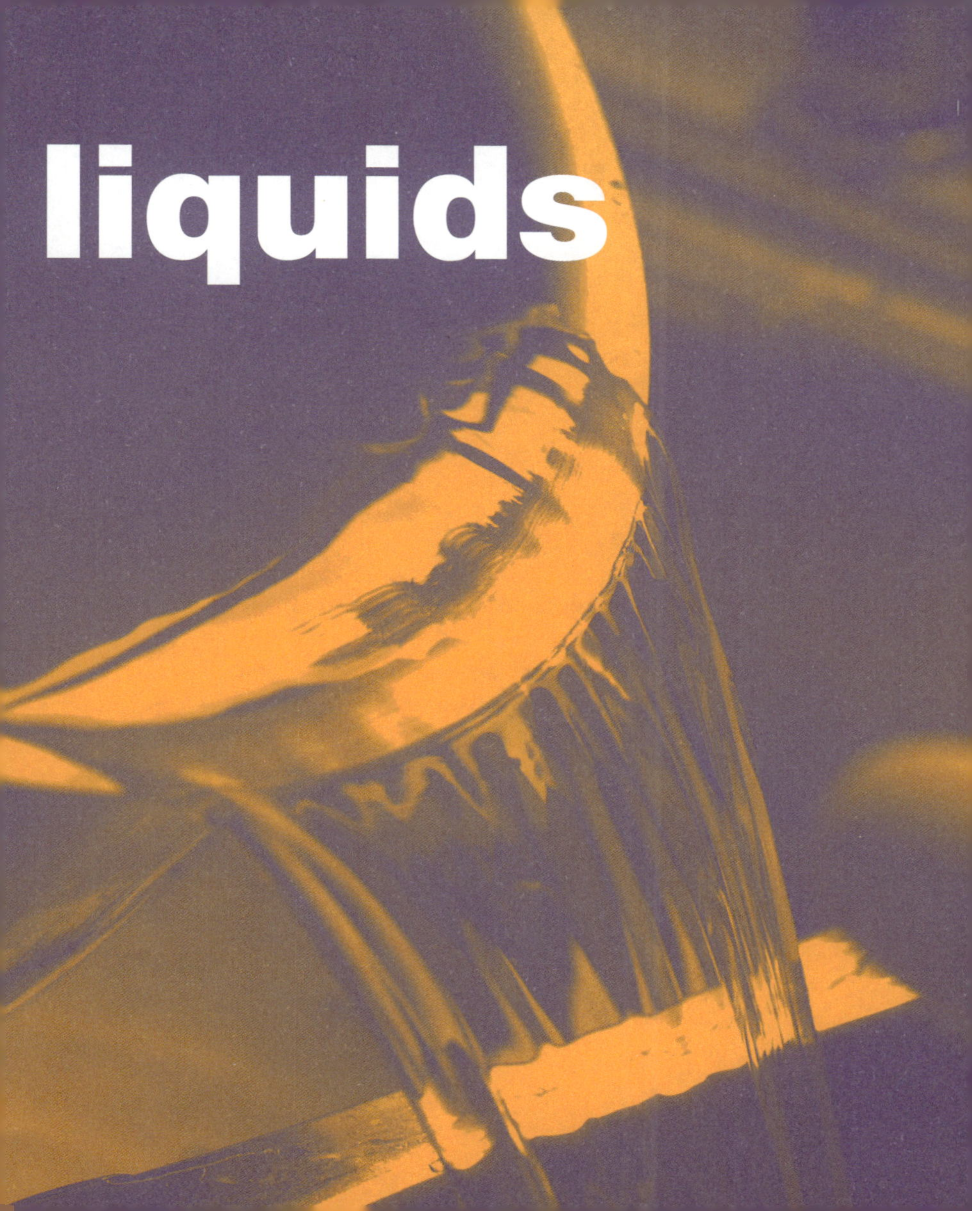

Mock
champagne

Can't wait till you're eighteen? Well don't worry, this is a great substitute for the real thing! You can make as much or as little as you want with this recipe.

1 part ginger ale
1 part apple juice
a few mint leaves

1 **Chill the ginger ale and apple juice in the fridge before preparing.**
2 **Mix together your desired amount.**
3 **Garnish with mint and serve.**

Hot caramel coffee

A great drink to help you stay up for those late Friday night movie marathons!
SERVES 2.

1 tablespoon instant coffee
2 cups hot milk
1/2 cup caramel flavouring
1/2 cup whipped cream
1 Violet Crumble bar, roughly chopped

1 **Place the instant coffee in a cup and add a tiny amount of boiling water – just enough to dissolve the coffee granules. Set aside.**
2 **Place the milk, flavouring and coffee syrup in a food processor and process for 10 seconds.**
3 **Pour the mixture into serving glasses and top with the cream and Violet Crumble pieces.**
4 **Serve immediately.**

Chockie nougat coffee

After you've had this drink I advise you to think about doing some exercise. Then again, you might be pretty hyperactive, so I won't have to advise you to do anything! SERVES 2.

50 g Toblerone pieces
2 cups prepared hot instant coffee
3/8 cup pouring cream
extra Toblerone to serve

1 **Break the Toblerone pieces into 2 medium-sized serving glasses.**
2 **Pour 1 cup of hot coffee into each glass. Stir until the Toblerone has melted.**
3 **Gently pour the cream on top. Serve straightaway with extra chocolate to eat with it.**

Choc-o-malt
thick shake

The secret to thick shakes is not to over-blend them, or they'll become milk shakes, but to blend them enough to avoid massive lumps of ice cream floating around. SERVES 2.

1 cup milk
a few scoops vanilla ice cream (the more you use, the thicker it'll be)
1 teaspoon maple syrup
$1/2$ cup drinking chocolate
$1/2$ cup powdered drinking malt

1 **Place the milk, ice cream and maple syrup in a food processor.**
2 **Add the drinking chocolate and malt.**
3 **Process on high for about 10 seconds, then on low for 15 seconds.**
4 **Pour into glasses and serve.**

Raspberry & strawberry smoothie

This'll help you get the girls or guys! Great for dates. SERVES 2.

300 g frozen raspberries, thawed until just soft
8 scoops vanilla ice cream
2 tablespoons raspberry or strawberry topping
1 Flake chocolate bar, roughly chopped

1 **Place the raspberries and ice cream into a food processor and process until smooth.**
2 **Pour the mixture into tall serving glasses and drizzle on the topping.**
3 **Sprinkle the Flake pieces on top or stir through. Serve.**

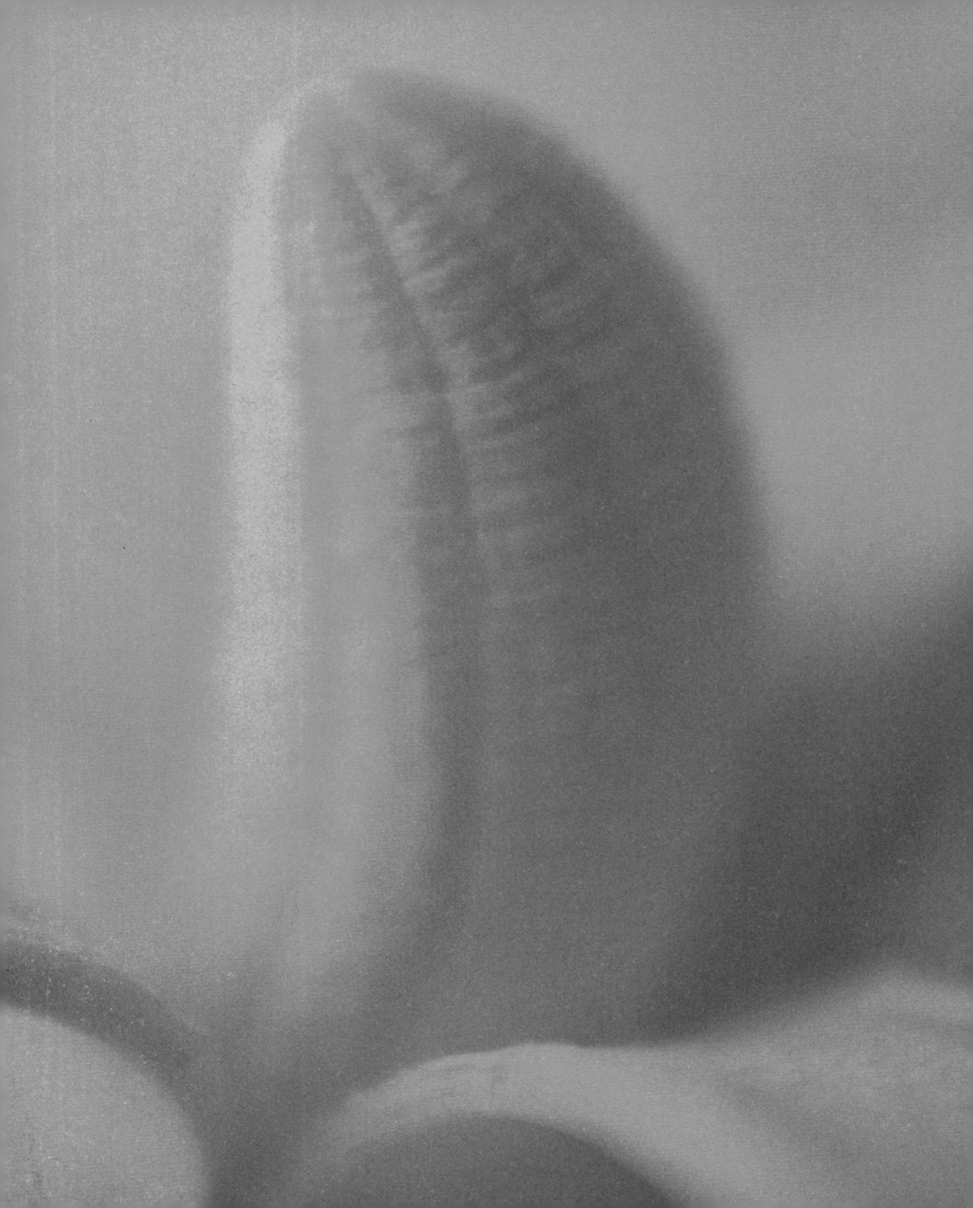

Banana
smoothie

Such a simple and popular drink, but it's rare to get one with just the
right flavour and consistency for the full Banana Smoothie Experience.
I created this recipe to get as close as possible to perfection. SERVES 2.

2 ripe bananas, peeled
2 scoops vanilla ice cream
1/2 cup milk
1 teaspoon honey
2 strawberries for garnish, split down the middle

**1 Place the bananas, ice cream, milk and honey in a
   food processor.**
**2 Process at medium speed for 30 seconds, or until
   smooth.**
**3 Serve in highball glasses and garnish each glass with
   a strawberry.**

Orange slush

Yeah, so maybe it's a little strange, but on a hot day you won't want to be doing anything else but drinking this! SERVES 4.

1/2 cup frozen yoghurt or ice cream
1 cup frozen orange juice concentrate, thawed
1/2 cup milk

1 **Place half the frozen yoghurt or ice cream, half the concentrate and half the milk in a food processor.**
2 **Cover and process at medium speed for about 45 seconds, stopping the food processor occasionally to scrape down the sides, until thick and smooth.**
3 **Add the remaining ingredients and repeat.**
4 **Pour the mixture into glasses and serve.**

feelin'
hungry

Mean banana porridge

This one is for brekkie – der! SERVES 2.

5 cups water
2¹/₂ cups quick oats
2 ripe bananas, peeled and sliced
1 teaspoon honey
¹/₂ cup soy or full cream milk (it's your choice!)
brown sugar to serve

1 Boil the water in a saucepan.
2 Add the oats and bananas and stir for about
   1 minute, or until the mixture thickens. Add the
   honey and stir.
3 When the water has completely evaporated, or the
   oats just begin to stick to the bottom of pan, remove
   from the heat.
4 Add the milk and stir, then allow to cool for about
   3 minutes.
5 Serve in bowls and sprinkle about 1 tablespoon of
   brown sugar over each serve.

French toast

This recipe is traditionally a breakfast meal, but it's nice anytime.
Try it with bacon or ice cream and maple syrup depending on whether
you feel like a sweet or savoury brekkie. SERVES 2.

2 eggs
$^1/_2$ cup milk
1 pinch cinnamon
4 slices white or wholemeal bread
20 g butter

**1 Whisk the eggs, milk and cinnamon in a bowl until
completely mixed.**
**2 Place the bread in the bowl, turning the slices over
so they get even coverage of the egg mixture and are
completely soaked through.**
**3 Melt half the butter in a large non-stick frying pan
over medium to high heat. Place 2 slices of the
soaked bread in the pan and fry for about 1 minute,
or until the bottom side is golden. Then, turn over
until the other side is golden.**
4 Repeat with the remaining butter and bread.
5 Serve with ice cream and maple syrup or bacon.

Pumpkin soup

An oldie but a goodie for fillin' the tummy! SERVES 2.

2 tablespoons vegetable oil
1 onion, finely chopped
3 cloves garlic, sliced
1 whole butternut pumpkin, cut into chunks
2 teaspoons ground ginger (optional)
300 ml chicken or vegetable stock
1 dollop cream or sour cream
chives, finely chopped, for garnish

1 Heat the oil over medium heat in a pot or pan with a lid. Fry the onion and garlic until soft.
2 Add the chopped pumpkin and ginger, if using. Stir for a couple of minutes, then add enough stock to just cover the pumpkin. Simmer with the lid off for 10–15 minutes, or until the mixture is cooked.
3 Process or mash the pumpkin until it's either slightly lumpy or smooth.
4 Stir through the sour cream or cream, then season with salt and pepper.
5 Serve with extra cream or sour cream and fresh-cut chives for a professional finish!

Speedy minestrone

Minestrone that's speedy! He he! SERVES 4.

1 teaspoon olive oil
1 medium carrot, coarsely chopped
1 stick celery, coarsely chopped
1 medium leek, coarsely chopped
3 rashers bacon, coarsely chopped
1 medium potato, coarsely chopped
2 x 400 g tins tomatoes
3 cups vegetable stock
1 1/2 L water
150 g small pasta shapes
300 g tin butter beans, drained and rinsed
1 cup frozen green beans, chopped

1 Heat the oil in a large saucepan. Cook the carrot, celery, leek, bacon and potato over medium heat, stirring, for about 7 minutes, or until the leek is soft.
2 Stir in the undrained tomatoes, stock and water. Bring to the boil and add the pasta. Simmer uncovered for about 10 minutes, or until the pasta is tender. Add the butter beans and green beans and simmer uncovered till heated through. Serve.

Roasted red
capsicum soup

Great in winter – just heat and eat! SERVES 4.

10 red capsicums
350 g tin of tomatoes
1 L chicken stock
1/2 cup almond meal
cayenne pepper

1 **Preheat the oven to 200°C.**
2 **Roast the capsicums on a baking tray for 30 minutes, or until the skin bubbles and darkens.**
3 **Remove the capsicums from the oven and leave in a covered bowl for 10 minutes, then peel carefully, discarding the skin and seeds.**
4 **Place the capsicum flesh and tomatoes in a food processor and process for about 2 minutes, or until smooth.**
5 **Pour the mixture through a sieve, pushing against the mesh to extract the maximum colour and flavour.**
6 **In a pot, combine the capsicum mixture and chicken stock and slowly add the almond meal, stirring continuously. Season with salt and cayenne pepper and serve hot.**

Caesar
salad

Caesar, eat your heart out. SERVES 4–6.

3 eggs
3 cloves garlic, crushed
4–6 anchovies, optional (or use as many as you like, but beware, they're strong!)
1 teaspoon Worcestershire sauce
2 tablespoons lime juice
1 teaspoon Dijon mustard
185 ml olive oil
4–6 slices white bread
30 g butter
4 rashers bacon
1 large or 4 baby cos lettuces
75 g shaved parmesan cheese

1 Process the eggs, garlic, anchovies, Worcestershire sauce, lime juice and mustard in a food processor until smooth. Add the oil slowly while blending to produce a creamy dressing.

2 Cut the crusts off the bread then cut the bread into small cubes. Heat the butter and a little extra olive oil in a frying pan over medium heat, add the bread cubes and cook for 5–8 minutes, or until crisp. Set them aside on paper towel.

3 In the same pan, cook the bacon for 3 minutes, or until crispy, then cut it into pieces.

4 Toss the lettuce leaves with the dressing, croutons and bacon. Top with parmesan cheese and serve.

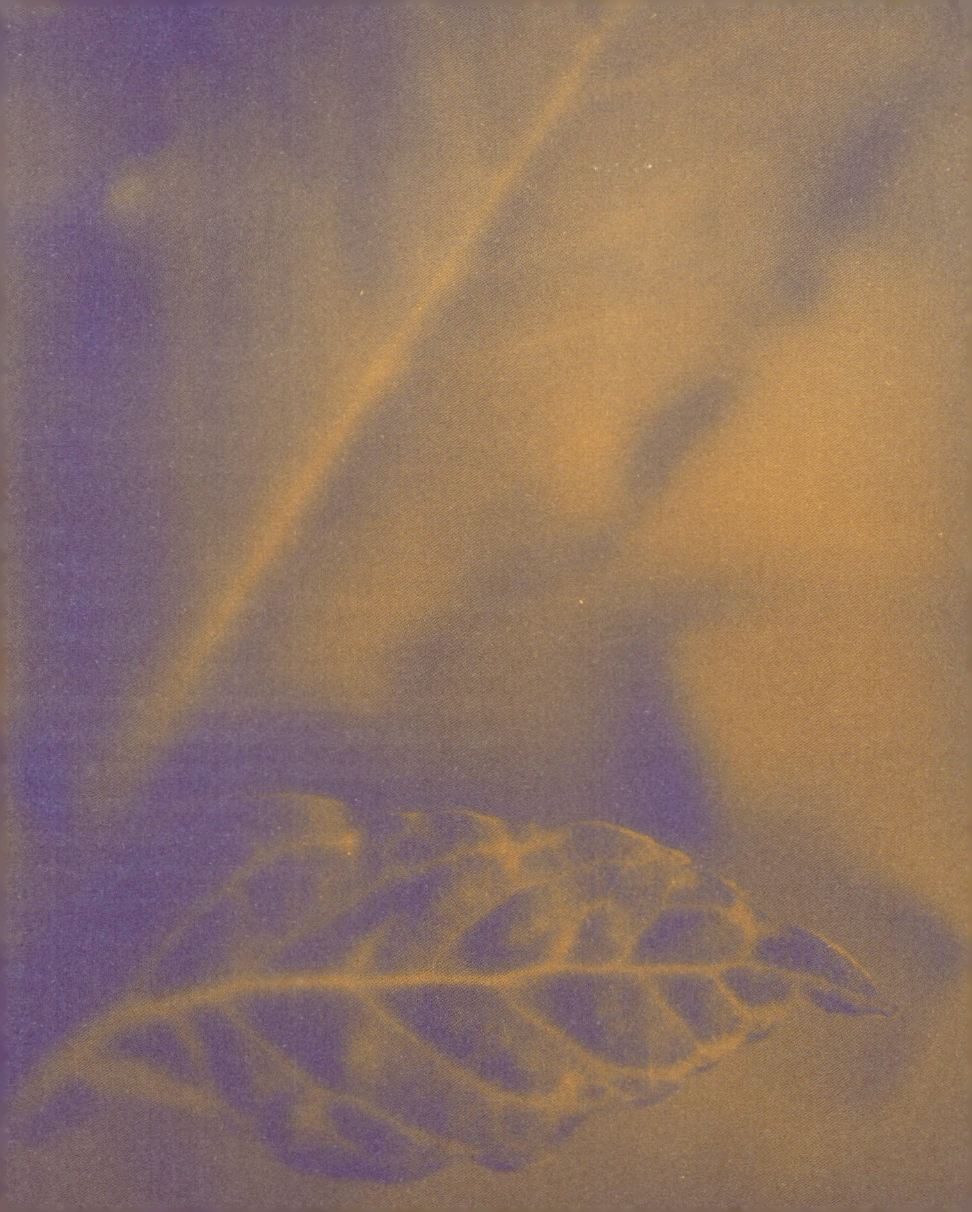

Easy
salad

Salads don't have to be a side dish – this one is nice by itself.
(Although there's nothing wrong with plonking a big fat steak next to it!)
SERVES 1.

4 button mushrooms
1 handful iceberg lettuce
1 handful rocket
1 small handful grated parmesan cheese
2 tablespoons vinegar-based salad dressing
1 small handful chopped parsley

1 Slice the mushrooms.
2 Combine all ingredients in a large bowl and mix well.
3 Serve.

Potato
salad

Not your ordinary spud salad. SERVES 10.

1 tablespoon oil
6 red onions, sliced
1 kg Kipfler or new potatoes, unpeeled
4 rashers streaky bacon, rind removed
30 g chives, chopped, plus extra for garnish

DRESSING
250 g whole-egg mayonnaise
1 tablespoon Dijon mustard
2 tablespoons sour cream
juice of 1 1/2 limes

1 Preheat the grill.

2 Heat the oil in a large frying pan. Add the onion and cook over low to medium heat for 15–20 minutes, or until soft and caramelised. Make sure it doesn't burn.

3 Cut the potatoes into large chunks. Cook in boiling water for 10 minutes, or until soft. Drain and allow to cool.

4 Grill the bacon until crisp, drain on paper towel and allow to cool before chopping coarsely.

5 Put the potato, onion and chives in a salad bowl and mix well.

6 For the dressing, put the whole-egg mayonnaise, mustard, sour cream and lime juice in a bowl and whisk to combine. Pour over the salad and toss to coat. Sprinkle with the bacon and garnish with extra chives. Serve.

Macaroni
cheese

Got some friends over? This is the perfect chill-out dish. Just stick it in the fridge if there's any left over. (There probably won't be.) SERVES 4.

2 cups macaroni
a splash olive oil
3 cups grated tasty cheese
1 1/2 cups grated Swiss cheese
1 cup thickened cream
2 eggs
30 g butter
1 cup fresh breadcrumbs
2 tomatoes, sliced (optional)
fresh basil leaves (optional)

1 Preheat the oven to 180°C.
2 Cook the macaroni in plenty of boiling, salted water according to the instructions on the packet. Add a splash of olive oil to the water to prevent sticking. Drain well.
3 Combine 2 cups of the tasty cheese, all the Swiss cheese, cream and eggs in a bowl. Mix in the macaroni. Spread half of the macaroni mixture in the base of a greased casserole dish.
4 Melt the butter in a frying pan. Add the breadcrumbs. Cook, stirring, for 5–7 minutes, or until the breadcrumbs are golden.
5 If using them, arrange the tomato slices and basil leaves over the macaroni layer. Top with the remaining macaroni mixture.
6 Combine the breadcrumbs and remaining tasty cheese. Sprinkle over the macaroni. Bake for about 15 minutes, or until golden.

Sun-dried tomato pasta

After making this recipe, you'll be the master of pasta! It's quick, it's easy, it's spectacular. SERVES 4.

500 g bowtie or penne pasta
50 g butter
1 onion, sliced
200 g jar sun-dried tomatoes, chopped
1/2 cup cream
2 tablespoons shredded basil, plus extra for garnish

1 **In a large saucepan, cook the pasta in boiling, salted water according to the instructions on the packet. Drain.**
2 **Melt the butter in a large frying pan over medium heat. Sauté the onion until soft.**
3 **Add the sun-dried tomatoes, cream and basil and season with salt and pepper. Reduce the heat and simmer for 3–5 minutes, or until the cream has reduced slightly.**
4 **Add the pasta to the pan and stir until it is mixed through. Garnish with extra basil and serve.**

Gnocchi
with pesto

Gnocchi goes well with anything but pesto is especially nice! It's light, simple and very very quick. SERVES 4.

500 g prepared gnocchi (If you don't have gnocchi you can use any pasta)
1 1/2 cups cream
1/2 cup prepared pesto sauce

1 **Cook the gnocchi in plenty of boiling water according to the instructions on the packet. Drain well in a colander and keep warm by covering the colander and sitting it over the hot water.**
2 **Bring the cream to the boil in a frying pan. Mix in the pesto sauce and season with pepper.**
3 **Toss the prepared gnocchi through the sauce. Heat, stirring, for 1 minute.**
4 **Serve immediately with crusty bread.**

Easy tuna pasta

Very nice indeed for those who like tuna. SERVES 2.

4 cups penne pasta
2 tablespoons olive oil
1 onion, chopped
185 g tin tuna
2 cups pasta sauce

1 Cook the pasta in plenty of boiling water according to the instructions on the packet. Drain and set aside.
2 While the pasta is cooking, heat the olive oil in a frying pan over high heat.
3 Reduce the heat to medium and add the onion. Fry for 2–3 minutes, or until soft.
4 Add the tuna and pasta sauce to the pan and allow the mixture to simmer on low to medium heat for 10 minutes.
5 Remove the sauce from the heat, allow to sit for about 10 minutes, then stir the pasta through the sauce. Season with salt and pepper and serve.

Tomato & bacon pasta sauce

This sauce can be served with either pasta or gnocchi, which you should cook according to the instructions on the packet while you prepare the sauce. SERVES 2–3.

1 tablespoon olive oil
1 onion, finely chopped
3 rashers bacon, roughly chopped
3–4 large fresh tomatoes, diced
4 basil leaves, finely chopped
1 pinch chilli

1 Heat the oil in a medium-sized frying pan. Sauté the onion until soft.
2 Add the bacon and cook until just crispy. Then add the tomatoes and basil and season with salt and pepper.
3 Turn down the heat to low and simmer for about 10 minutes, or until the tomatoes become mushy. If the sauce becomes a bit dry while cooking, add a bit of water or olive oil.
4 Add the chilli and stir through. Serve immediately with pasta.

Pin-wheel
pizzas

This version of pizza is dynamite. MAKES 10 PIN-WHEELS,
OR SERVES 2 AS A MAIN MEAL.

1 sheet pre-made frozen puff pastry
tomato paste
1 onion, finely chopped
$^1/_2$ cup finely chopped parsley
$^1/_2$ cup finely chopped ham
$^1/_2$ cup grated cheese
Optional toppings: avocado, spinach, mushroom, pineapple,
salami

1 **Preheat the oven to 220°C.**
2 **Lay out the sheets of pastry to thaw.**
3 **Spread a layer of tomato paste over the pastry.**
   Sprinkle on the other ingredients and any optional
   extras and cover with grated cheese.
4 **Roll up the pastry and seal the ends with milk or**
   water. Cut it into about 10 pieces.
5 **Lay the pieces on their sides on an oven tray and**
   bake for 15 minutes. Serve.

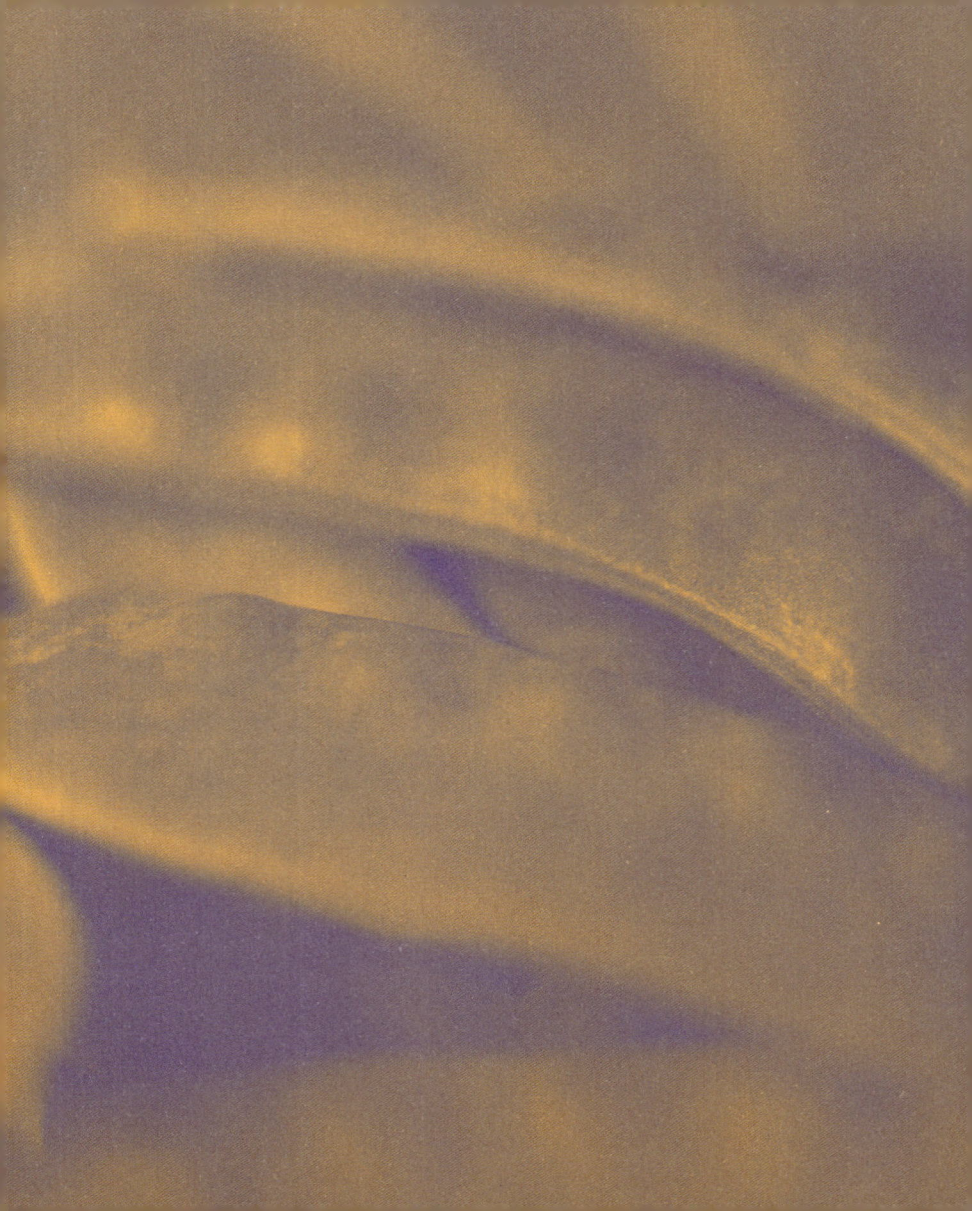

Coconut curry

This curry is so good you'll need to be careful who you serve it to. They just might start turning up at your place around dinnertime. SERVES 4.

3 tablespoons red curry paste
6 chicken thigh fillets, halved
10 snow peas
2 cups cubed sweet potato
2 cups chicken stock
1$^{1}/_{2}$ cups coconut milk
$^{1}/_{2}$ cup coriander leaves

1 Warm a frying pan over medium heat and add the curry paste. Cook for 1–2 minutes, or until the paste is fragrant. Add the chicken, snow peas and sweet potato to the pan and cook for 2 minutes.
2 Add the stock and coconut milk and reduce the heat to low. Simmer gently for 12 minutes or until the chicken and sweet potato are cooked through.
3 Sprinkle the coriander over the chicken and serve with steamed rice.

Chicken laksa

As for any Asian recipe, make sure you use fresh ingredients for this one. It may be a drag but the difference is massive. SERVES 4.

$1/2$ cup laksa or green curry paste
400 g chicken fillets, thinly sliced
1 tablespoon oil
500 ml chicken stock
400 ml coconut milk
10 pieces baby corn
1 bunch bok choy, sliced
200 g dried rice vermicelli noodles
sliced red capsicum for garnish

1 Combine 1 teaspoon of laksa paste with the chicken and mix well.

2 Heat a wok or large saucepan over high heat. Add 2 teaspoons of oil and half the chicken to the wok and stir-fry for 1 minute, or until seared. Remove, cover and set aside. Repeat with the remaining oil and chicken and set aside.

3 Add the remaining laksa paste to the same wok and stir-fry for about 1 minute. Stir in the stock and coconut milk. Bring to the boil, stirring occasionally.

4 Reduce the heat to medium-low and add the chicken, baby corn and bok choy. Cover and simmer for 5 minutes, or until the chicken is cooked through.

5 Cook the noodles in a saucepan of boiling salted water until just tender. Drain and separate the noodles into bowls. Ladle the soup over the noodles. Top with sliced red capsicum and serve.

Chicken
fried rice

Fried rice without the grease of takeaways, but with the knowledge of where it came from and what's in it! SERVES 4.

1 onion, diced
1 clove garlic, finely diced
1 red capsicum, chopped
2 carrots, chopped
1 stick celery, chopped
1 handful beans, chopped
1 handful snow peas, chopped
4 cups cooked white rice
soy sauce and sweet soy sauce, to taste
2 cooked chicken breasts, coarsely shredded

1 Heat some oil in a wok or large pot over medium heat. Sauté the onion and garlic for about 5 minutes. Add all the other vegies and stir-fry, adding a few splashes of soy sauce, for 10 minutes, or until just tender.
2 Add the cooked rice and mix well. Add the soy and sweet soy sauces to taste. Finally, add the chicken, mixing well through the rice. Heat until everything is warmed through.
3 Yummy with a bit of sweet chilli sauce, too. Serve.

Plum pork steaks

Sometimes you want a good ol' slab of barbecued meat but you also want something new. Marinating things is the answer – so simple, but makes such a difference. This recipe is just what you need to make a boring meal into a gourmet one. SERVES 4.

1/2 cup plum sauce
1 tablespoon Worcestershire sauce
1 tablespoon honey
1 tablespoon oil
1 clove garlic, finely chopped
1 small red chilli, deseeded and finely chopped
4 pork scotch steaks

1 Preheat the barbecue.
2 To make the marinade, combine the sauces, honey, oil, garlic and chilli in a jug and stir.
3 Place the steaks in a shallow dish and pour the marinade over them. Turn the steaks to coat them in marinade. Cover the dish with plastic wrap and refrigerate for 30–40 minutes.
4 Barbecue the steaks over high heat, basting regularly with the marinade, for 10–12 minutes, or until they are just cooked through. Serve immediately.

Pork Madras

Just the thing when you want yummy curry in a damn hurry! SERVES 4.

4 rashers bacon, coarsely chopped
1 tablespoon peanut oil
700 g pork fillets, thinly sliced
1 large white onion, thinly sliced
$^1/_2$ cup Madras curry paste (or any curry paste you like)
100 g snake beans, coarsely chopped
100 g green beans, coarsely chopped
$^1/_2$ cup beef stock
1 tablespoon tomato paste
$^1/_2$ cup chopped coriander

1 **In a hot dry wok or pan, stir-fry the bacon, stirring constantly, until crisp. This won't take long. Then allow it to drain on paper towel.**
2 **Heat the oil in the same wok. Stir-fry the pork and onion for a few minutes, or until browned. Set aside.**
3 **Stir-fry the curry paste in the same wok until just fragrant. Add the snake and green beans to the wok with the pork mixture, bacon, stock and tomato paste. Stir through the coriander. Stir-fry continuously until the sauce boils.**
4 **Remove from the heat immediately and serve on rice with a sprinkle of coriander.**

Rack of lamb

You just can't eat this one without mashed potatoes. SERVES 2.

2 small racks lamb
4 cloves garlic
2 sprigs rosemary
olive oil

1 **Preheat the oven to 200°C.**
2 **Prepare the meat by scoring• the large piece of fat nearly down to the meat.**
3 **Make small holes all over the meat** (about four holes per rack) **then stick half a clove of garlic and a piece of rosemary into each hole.**
4 **Cover the ends of the bones with foil. Sprinkle oil over the meat and season with cracked pepper and salt.**
5 **Lean the racks against each other in a well-greased baking dish, the bones pointing upwards, and roast in the oven for 20–30 minutes** (depending on how rare or well done you want the meat). **Serve immediately with mashed potatoes.**

• Scoring means slicing the surface of the fat in a criss-cross pattern. Don't do it too deep or too shallow – it should be just deep enough that it doesn't cut into the meat.

Ma Jill's Hi Ti Ming

I got this recipe from my dad, who says his mum, Jill, used to make it all the time. Now Dad makes it as well, but I wish he'd refer to the recipe and not make his own version! Don't worry though – this is Jill's exact recipe, not Dad's! SERVES 4.

500 g mince
2 onions, chopped
1 packet chicken noodle soup
2 teaspoons curry powder
1/2 cup rice
2 sticks celery, chopped
2 cups water
1/2 cabbage, sliced

1 **Fry the mince and onion together in a saucepan with a lid, over medium to high heat.**
2 **Add the contents of the chicken noodle soup packet, curry powder, rice, celery and water. Simmer with the lid on for 15 minutes.**
3 **Stir the cabbage through and simmer with the lid on for a few minutes until the cabbage is soft. Serve.**

Fish cakes

This is a great recipe for any non-seafood fans. SERVES 4.

700 g white boneless fish, chopped
(or if you can't get fish, canned salmon
or tuna will suffice)
2 eggs, lightly whisked
1/2 cup dried breadcrumbs
2 tablespoons parsley, finely chopped
2 tablespoons olive oil

1 **Combine the fish, eggs, breadcrumbs
and parsley in a large bowl. Season
with salt and pepper.**
2 **Divide the mixture into eight equal
portions and shape into patties.**
3 **Heat the oil in a large, non-stick frying
pan over medium heat. Add the patties
and cook for 3–4 minutes on each side,
or until golden brown. Serve immediately.**

Vegetarian noodles

Good as a side dish or as a meal. If you want to add meat, throw it in at stage 2 and stir-fry till cooked. SERVES 4.

1 packet rice stick noodles (or any thin rice noodles)
6 button mushrooms, thinly sliced (optional)
soy sauce
3 carrots, grated
2 zucchinis, grated
1 handful green beans, chopped into very small pieces
crushed peanuts, to taste

1 **Cook the rice stick noodles in plenty of boiling water according to the instructions on the packet. Rinse them in cold water and set aside.**
2 **In a pan over medium heat, sauté the mushrooms in a little butter for 3 minutes, adding a little soy sauce for taste.**
3 **Place the noodles into a large serving dish, separating them as you go. Add all the veggies and toss until mixed through. Add soy sauce to taste.**
4 **Sprinkle crushed peanuts over the top and serve.**

Spanish omelette

Good at any time of day, this is the most diverse recipe in the book.
Put in whatever ingredients you think will be nice. You don't have to
use the ones I've given you, but I would! SERVES 2.

- **1 teaspoon butter**
- **1 small onion, chopped**
- **1 clove garlic, minced**
- **2 rashers bacon, chopped**
- **1 cup fresh chopped vegetables** (eg, pre-boiled
  and cubed potatoes, capsicum, tomato, celery, corn)
- **6 eggs, whisked together**
- **1/2 cup fresh chopped herbs of choice**
- **1 handful grated cheese**

1. **Melt the butter in a large frying pan. Sauté the onion, garlic and bacon until the onion is soft.**
2. **Add the vegetables and stir-fry for 5–6 minutes.**
3. **Pour the eggs and herbs over the vegetables, making sure the egg mixture is evenly covering the pan.**
4. **Sprinkle the cheese over the top and cook over medium heat for about 5 minutes, or until the edges look cooked. Place the frying pan under the grill for 2–5 minutes, or until the top is brown. Serve.**

The bomb burritos

These burritos, man, are the bomb! SERVES 2.

1 tablespoon oil
1 onion, diced
400 g tin three bean mix or red kidney beans
400 g tin crushed tomatoes
2 burritos
$1/2$ avocado
1 fresh tomato, sliced
sour cream
cheese, sliced or grated

1 Heat the oil in a frying pan over high heat. Add the onion and fry until slightly brown.
2 Add the beans and tinned tomatoes. Simmer for 5 minutes, then remove the mixture from the heat and let cool.
3 Place one burrito on a plate and add some bean mix, avocado, sliced tomato, sour cream and cheese. Fold the sides of the burrito in and roll it up.
4 Toast in the grill until brown. Repeat with the remaining burrito and serve.

sweet
thangs

Caramel
sauce

This is to die for. You can bottle any excess and stick it in the fridge for next time. It will last about a week. MAKES ABOUT 250 ML OF SAUCE.

30 g butter
1/2 cup maple syrup
1 tablespoon cream

1 **Melt the butter in a frying pan. Stir in the maple syrup and allow to simmer for 2–3 minutes, or until completely mixed.**
2 **Add the cream, stir and allow to simmer for about 5 minutes, or until completely mixed. Then remove from the heat immediately.**
3 **Serve hot on ice cream.**

Banana &
choc melts

These are great thrown on a campfire or barbecue. SERVES AS MANY AS YOU LIKE.

**your choice of chocolate, about 1 family block
    for 4 bananas
as many bananas as you want, unpeeled**

1 **Preheat the oven to 220°C.**
2 **Crush or finely chop the chocolate into a bowl or on a chopping board.**
3 **With a sharp knife, cut a flap about 2 centimetres wide down the length of each banana skin.**
4 **Scoop out as much banana as required to make a trench. Fill with the crushed or chopped chocolate.**
5 **Close the skin flap back over and wrap the banana in foil.**
6 **Bake for about 30 minutes.**
7 **Carefully remove the bananas from the oven and let stand for 5 minutes, then remove the foil and serve with ice cream or cream.**

Watermelon sorbet

This is refreshing, more-ish, and great to chill out with. Love it!
Careful you don't get 'brain freeze'… SERVES 4.

1 cup water
1 cup caster sugar
1¹/₂ kg watermelon, rind removed and cut into chunks

1 **Place the sugar and water in a saucepan and stir over low heat until the sugar has dissolved.**
2 **Bring to the boil, then reduce the heat and simmer for 5 minutes. Pour into a bowl and allow to cool.**
3 **Process the watermelon in a food processor and strain to remove the seeds.**
4 **Stir the sugar syrup into the watermelon purée and pour into a shallow metal dish. Freeze for 1 hour then stir well with a fork. Repeat this step 2 or 3 more times, then serve. Note: you shouldn't leave sorbet in the freezer without stirring it every hour.**

Simple chocolate cake

Just the best chocolate cake ever – that's it! MAKES 1 CAKE.

2 cups plain flour
2 cups caster sugar
1 cup cocoa
1 teaspoon bicarbonate of soda
2 teaspoons baking powder
$1/2$ teaspoon salt
$2/3$ cup butter, melted
2 eggs
2 cups boiling water
2 teaspoons of vanilla essence

1 Preheat the oven to 180°C.
2 Combine all the dry ingredients in a bowl. Mix well.
3 In another bowl, combine the butter, eggs, boiling water and vanilla. Mix the wet and dry ingredients well. Make sure all the lumps in the mixture are gone before you pour it into a well-greased cake tin.
4 Bake in the oven for 20 minutes.
5 Put any type of icing you like on this cake, or just dust with icing sugar. Serve with cream or ice cream.

Raspberry & pavlova ice cream cake

You might have to buy a tub of Clearasil after pigging out on this one!
(But go on, make it, you know you want to!) MAKES 1 CAKE.

- **1 L vanilla ice cream**
- **1 L wildberry sorbet**
- **1 packet already-made pavlova** (you can get these in supermarkets or cake shops)
- **1 packet frozen raspberries or 1 punnet fresh raspberries**

1 **Mix the ice cream, sorbet and pavlova together in a large bowl.**
2 **Base a thick large metal mixing bowl** (you can use a plastic one if you don't have a metal one) **with plastic wrap to prevent sticking. Then cover the base with raspberries.**
3 **Pour the ice cream mixture over the raspberries and place the bowl in the freezer, preferably overnight. Serve when the ice cream has set.**

Glazed
apple tart

Be careful with this recipe, it's a bit tricky. But very impressive!
SERVES 4.

$1/3$ cup caster sugar
$2^1/2$ tablespoons water
50 g unsalted butter, softened
2 tablespoons brown sugar
$1/2$ teaspoon ground cinnamon
$1/2$ teaspoon finely grated lemon rind
2 tablespoons finely chopped nuts
4 apples, peeled and thickly sliced
2 sheets puff pastry

1 Preheat the oven to 200°C.

2 To make the toffee, combine the caster sugar and water in a small saucepan. Stir over low heat until the sugar has dissolved. Boil uncovered without stirring for about 5 minutes, or until the syrup is golden brown. Pour the toffee into a greased 20-centimetre sandwich tin (this is the smallest cake tin). Tilt to cover the base evenly.

3 Beat the butter, brown sugar, cinnamon and lemon rind in a small bowl until the mixture is light and fluffy. Stir in the nuts. Spoon small dollops of this mixture over the toffee in the tin. Arrange the apple slices over the top.

4 Place one pastry sheet on top of the other. Cut the pastry into a circle slightly larger than the pan. Prick all over with a fork. Lift and place over the tin, tucking the edges down over the sides. Bake for about 30 minutes or until the pastry is puffed and crisp.

5 Stand for 10 minutes before turning out onto a serving plate. Serve with cream or ice cream.

Marshmallow slice

Get ready for this one because it makes a devastating mess. Well worth it, though. MAKES 24 PIECES OF SLICE.

1 cup self-raising flour, sifted
1 cup desiccated coconut
1/2 cup brown sugar
1 Weet-bix, crushed
180 g butter, melted
2 tablespoons raspberry jam
375 g packet assorted marshmallows

1 Preheat the oven to 180°C.
2 Combine the flour, coconut, sugar and Weet-bix in a large bowl. Pour in the melted butter, mixing well.
3 Press the mixture into a rectangular lamington tin. Bake for about 20–25 minutes.
4 Remove from the oven and spread jam over the surface while still hot. Arrange the marshmallows close together on top. Bake for another 10 minutes.
5 Allow to cool. Cut into squares. Serve, or store in an airtight container.

Choc chip cookies

This recipe was given to me by my good friends Mia and Ash, and I know these cookies are yum because every time they make them they're quickly stolen by an anonymous person … MAKES ABOUT 18 COOKIES.

125 g butter, softened
1/3 cup caster sugar
1/3 cup brown sugar
1 egg
1/2 teaspoon vanilla essence
2 teaspoons maple syrup
1 1/2 cups plain flour
1/2 teaspoon bicarbonate of soda
1/2 teaspoon salt
100 g milk chocolate melts
100 g white chocolate melts

1 Preheat the oven to 190°C.
2 Mix the butter, caster suger and brown sugar in a bowl until creamy. Add the egg and beat until smooth, then add the vanilla essence and maple syrup.
3 A bit at a time, add the flour, bicarbonate of soda and salt to the butter mixture and stir well. Add all the chocolate and stir until it is evenly combined.
4 Grease a baking tray and spoon small amounts of mixture onto it, leaving about 2 centimetres between each cookie.
5 Bake for 10–12 minutes until the cookies are a golden brown colour, then remove from the oven and allow to cool. Now quick, eat them, before someone else does!

Coconut pancakes with watermelon

After this you'll always know how to make great pancakes. SERVES 6.

1/3 cup shredded coconut
1 2/3 cup plain flour
2 teaspoons baking powder
2 tablespoons caster sugar
2 fresh free-range eggs
2 cups milk
1 tablespoon butter, melted
750 g watermelon, peeled, diced and deseeded
honey to serve

1 Place the coconut in a dry frying pan for toasting over low heat. Cook, stirring, for 3–4 minutes, or until golden brown. Remove and let stand for 5 minutes.

2 Sift the flour and baking powder into a medium-sized bowl. Mix in the coconut and sugar.

3 In a separate bowl, whisk the eggs and milk together. Make a well in the flour mixture then, a little at a time, combine the egg mixture until a smooth batter is formed. Stir in the melted butter and transfer the batter to a large jug.

4 Lightly grease a non-stick frying pan over medium heat. Pour $1/2$ cup of batter into the pan to make a 12-centimetre pancake. Cook for 2–3 minutes, or until bubbles rise to the surface and the pancake is golden underneath. Turn with a spatula and cook for a further 1–2 minutes. Remove and cover with foil to keep warm.

5 Repeat with the remaining batter, greasing the pan if necessary, to make 12 pancakes.

6 To serve, stack 2 pancakes on a plate and top with the watermelon. Drizzle honey over the top to serve.

Mars Bar slice

One of the most scrumptious snacks and dead easy as well! SERVES 4.

90 g butter
3 Mars Bars, broken into small pieces
3 cups Rice Bubbles
250 g milk chocolate, broken into pieces

1 Place the butter and Mars Bar pieces in a microwave-safe bowl and heat in the microwave until the butter is melted. Stir to form a sludgy consistency.
2 Stir in the Rice Bubbles until completely mixed through.
3 Place baking paper in a shallow baking tray and pour in the mixture. Put in the fridge.
4 Place the chocolate pieces in a bowl and microwave on high until they are almost melted. This should take 3–4 minutes, but keep checking. Remove and then stir until smooth.
5 Remove the slice from the fridge and spread the chocolate on top, then allow it to cool in the fridge for another minute.
6 Cut into slices and eat with hot chocolate.

Rocky road

This sinfully wicked treat disappears faster than it's made, and trust me, it's a pretty quick one to make! MAKES 2 SERVES.

1/2 cup choc melts
1/2 packet copha, roughly chopped
6 marshmallows
1/2 cup unsalted peanuts
1/2 cup shredded coconut
1/2 cup raspberry lollies

1 Place a bowl over a saucepan of boiling water. Add the choc melts and copha and allow them to melt.
2 When melted, take the chocolate mixture off the heat and add the marshmallows, peanuts, coconut and raspberry lollies. Stir until the dry ingredients are covered, then spread over the base of a plastic container and leave in the fridge to cool.
3 When the mixture has solidified, press it out of the container and cut into desired pieces.

Anzac biscuits

Instead of your grandma bringing you Anzac biscuits, you can make them and take them to her! MAKES 15–20 BISCUITS.

1 cup plain flour
1 cup desiccated coconut
$2/3$ cup brown sugar
1 cup rolled oats
$1/2$ cup crushed almonds
125 g butter
1 tablespoon golden syrup
$1/2$ teaspoon bicarbonate of soda
2 tablespoons boiling water

1 Preheat the oven to 160°C.
2 Combine the flour, coconut, sugar, oats and almonds in a bowl and mix well.
3 Place the butter and golden syrup in a saucepan over medium heat and melt.
4 Place the bicarbonate of soda in a small bowl and add the water. Stir to combine, then pour it into the butter mixture and stir. Pour the combined mixture over the dry ingredients and stir through.
5 Roll teaspoons of biscuit mixture into balls and place on a greased and lined baking tray. Flatten each ball.
6 Bake for 15–20 minutes, or until the biscuits are golden brown.

index

First published 2003 in Pan by Pan Macmillan Australia
Pty Limited
St Martins Tower, 31 Market Street, Sydney

National Library of Australia
Cataloguing-in-Publication data:

Farriss, Jake.
The teenager's survival cookbook.

ISBN 0 330 36444 8.

I. Cookery. 2. Quick and easy cookery. I. Title.

641.512

Typeset in Helvetica by Seymour Designs
Printed in Australia by Ligare Book Printers
Cover and text design by Seymour Designs
Cover photograph by Katrina Crook
Internal photographs by Digitalvision, Getty and Katrina Crook